Why We Hurt

Why We Hurt

by

john dishwasher

six fires.press

The background on the cover and the "bird man" figure below the cover's title are from Lascaux Cave, dated to about 17,000 years ago. The figure on the opposite page is 'The Sorcerer' from the cave of the Trois-Frères, dated to about 15,000 years ago. Both caves are in southwestern France.

This essay was first conceived and drafted in Worcester, MA, 2007. Major revisions pointing to the final version were made in Richmond, VA, 2014. The final draft was executed in Murrieta, CA, 2021. Version 1 was copyrighted September 2023. This book is Version 2, published by Six Fires Press on February 1, 2026. These contents are 100% human-created.

ISBN: 979-8-9860184-2-3
ISBN ebook: 979-8-9860184-1-6

part one

The Rift

Elizabeth feels empty. Something is missing inside her. A wrongness there. She distracts herself from the hurt with amusements, with friends, with narcotics, with work. But then her friends leave. Or she powers down her laptop. Or she wakes up from her binge. Or quietly she recuperates on the sofa after a long noisy barista shift. Elizabeth sits alone then, solitary, apart from the busyness of her life; without diversion or stimuli, without even an essay like this to contemplate. And Elizabeth feels empty.

Elizabeth's emptiness is universal. Elizabeth's story is ever-present. If you can read these words, you know what she is feeling. We all feel empty sometimes, and we all marshal considerable cleverness and energy to deflect away those barren minutes when we feel empty. I have written this essay to describe why you and I and Elizabeth feel empty.

Some authors have portrayed this emptiness we feel as foundational to the human condition, suggesting that its universality among us implies it is integral to us and so inescapable. While in commoner cases, like Elizabeth's and mine, this conclusion seems incontrovertible; importantly, there are exceptional cases that rebut it. A few humans in our history have eluded the dark feelings of this emptiness we all experience. Their escape has been so unequivocal, and the wholeness and peace they enjoyed by that escape so evident, that we have come to hail them as prophets, messiahs, world teachers, spiritual messengers. Many have tried to imbibe the teachings these wise ones left behind and by their guidance achieve the wholeness and peace they embodied. I do not publish this essay to contradict these teachings, but to com-plement them. Each of those personalities left us a path toward the wholeness they exampled. But none explained in modern terms why we lack that wholeness in the first place.

My thesis is simple: Over eons humans evolved to interact with the world in one way, but over recent millennia humans have been trained to interact with the world in a different way. The disconnect between how we evolved to interact with the world and how we are now trained to interact with the world creates a schism within us, a rift. When we feel empty we are feeling that rift.

To support this thesis I will demonstrate that our eldest ancestors exercised a psychology very different from our modern psychology and that only relatively recently our ancestors transitioned out of that original psychology. I will also show that this event transformed how we humans relate to the world around us. We will see that the simultaneous loss of our original psychology and our original relationship with the world is crucial to understanding our emptiness; and that in prehistory we can discern when and even how the change occurred. Then, coming forward from there, we will see how this seismic shift has complicated our mental, emotional, and spiritual lives since.

By the time you finish reading this essay you will be able to source the emptiness that Elizabeth and you and I share to a prehistoric era tens of thousands of years ago. Also you will have an understanding of the wholeness of our ancestors' original psychology, of how it still dwells within each of us today, and that it can be reclaimed.

To reclaim that original psychology and its wholeness will lead us back to the paths described by the various prophets and messiahs and world teachers who have inspired so many to emulate them. Informed now by our modern explanation of why we lack their wholeness in the first place, we will see that each of those wise ones, through their own particular spirituality, simply found a different way to reclaim our original psychology.

Elizabeth

So meet Elizabeth. Today is an unusual school day for her. It is a Wednesday in April and she is scheduled to deliver an informative presentation to her speech class. As we catch up with Elizabeth she is gassing her rattly old sedan down the freeway toward her urban college campus. The dashboard clock says 7 a.m. We watch Elizabeth shift gears, engage her turn signal, and weave among vehicles as she navigates traffic. She arrives, parks her car, and tugs her favorite knit cap off her broad brow as she strides into the student union. There

Elizabeth sips at a mug of coffee and bends over her phone, mentally rehearsing the speech she will soon perform. Elizabeth is a twenty-something woman of average height and average build. She has an affable personality, a non-serious boyfriend with whom she shares occasional weekend outings, and a recently rescued cat named Captain. Her wavy hair and large eyes are of profound brown. Deliberately this morning Elizabeth dressed unexceptionally in khakis and a black polo shirt with fine red stripes, aiming to draw as little attention to her appearance as possible while standing before her peers.

After a couple of run-throughs Elizabeth checks the time. Her palms suddenly dampen with nervous sweat. She rises from the cafeteria table and tensely tracks out of the student union and to her classroom, arriving about ten minutes early. The instructor puts the class in motion soon and her turn comes up. Elizabeth assumes the podium. By manipulating the computer's mouse she projects images onto the screen behind her – ancient cave paintings of African bison and kudu. As she speaks she intersperses humorous metaphors and colorful vocabulary into her presentation and modulates her volume and enuncia-

[17]

tion in order to disguise her fright. Finally Elizabeth's moments in the spotlight end. She sidles from the lectern to take again her desk. She exhales. The film of anxious perspiration that plagued her throughout the speech now collects into rolling beads that cascade over her broad brow. But Elizabeth is relieved. At last she has completed this rather onerous assignment required for a passing grade. Soon, she expects, she will graduate and commence the next phase of her life.

As straightforward as this portrait of Elizabeth may appear, it actually somewhat deceives. For the elements here most

[18]

pertinent to the argument of this essay are not those we casually recognize in Elizabeth, but those we habitually over-look. Though I have intentionally em-phasized some suggestive aspects of her physicality and mentality, probably none of them reminded you that, at root, Elizabeth is an animal. Rarely do we consider this about each other, or our-selves. But even there at the head of her college classroom, dressed in the fashion of her day, managing the sophisticated machinery of modern times, and literally miles and miles distant from any kind of natural setting, still Elizabeth is a part of nature's continuum. If carefully we examine where Elizabeth fits on nature's continuum, but also where she transcends it, we will take our first step toward comprehending why you and I and Elizabeth feel empty.

Difference of Expression

First, where Elizabeth fits.

Each of the physical aspects historically argued to be unique to human beings is more or less visible as Elizabeth fidgets there before her fellow undergraduates. She carries an extremely large brain relative to body size as she nods toward the screen behind her. We see miniaturized hair across her arms which leaves the skin exposed as she waves backward. When Elizabeth lifts her hand to gesture her armpits show a dampness. This signals her potential for profuse sweating. As she grips the mouse we don't really notice, despite its import, the dexterity made possible by thumbs which can oppose any other digit on her hands. And though Elizabeth stands at that podium during her speech, we've seen how she can also walk on those two legs of hers. To facilitate this her feet are arched and buttressed, her lower limbs are long and strong, her pelvis rounded and flared, and her head rests vertically upon the vertebral column. And perhaps what most interests us, and definitely what primarily commands our attention, is that Elizabeth can articulate sounds into speech. The parabolic shape of her mouth makes this possible, along with the arch of her basicranium, and the fact her larynx sits low in her throat, making the sound chamber, or pharynx, large in relative terms and conducive to a wide range of sounds.

These several traits of Elizabeth's physicality are her most salient when compared to the rest of the animal kingdom. Some are so striking, in fact, that at different times in history, scientists have cited one or the other as singular, as the unique physical detail which sets her and other human beings apart from the natural world. And yet none of these bodily attributes are wholly exclusive to us. For example, all mammals share a form of the larynx, pharynx, tongue, and lips that Elizabeth exercises to articulate the words of her report. Elephants, rhinoceros, and the naked mole rat each match our hairlessness. Dolphins enjoy exceptionally large brains relative to body size. Horses sweat. Other primates employ fingers and thumbs. And Ostriches and penguins even walk upright, though of course not with the graceful gait Elizabeth exhibited upon approaching the podium.

As we watch Elizabeth bravely chiming on there about the lumpy transition from one era of consciousness to another, therefore, and symbolizing for us our entire human race, she does not stand exactly unique on the face of planet Earth. Every trait she displays that might suggest her physically singular as a homo sapien she shares with some other Earthly species, even those profound brown eyes of hers. So it is not the bodily attributes of the human being, considered individually, which make humans unique among all the species; but rather the particular *combination* of these attributes and their particular *expression* which make human beings unique. But the same can be said for the kangaroo.

Difference of Degree

If we turn our attention away from how Elizabeth appears and toward how she thinks, her position within nature's continuum becomes more suspect. For Elizabeth's mentality is extraordinary. Its many gifts impress. The extent to which she can generate and interpret symbols, think abstractly, and formulate the strategies she employs to communicate her presentation effectively and persuasively seems definitive. But when Elizabeth applies these capacities to her mentality itself something even more marvelous kindles: Introspection, and an acute awareness of self. Over the centuries different thinkers have indicated one or another of these mental gifts as the principal element which separates humans from nature. Still others have pointed to the social manifestations which arise from them, like culture, or symbolic behavior, or morality. Scientific investigation has demonstrated, however, that homo sapiens are not as isolated in any of these modes of being as once believed. Chimpanzees may not fret over what clothes to wear before their peers, but experiments ferreting out basic proofs of self-awareness in them show they exercise it, and culture is clearly evident among them; and their ability to use language (which is our most poignant form of symbolic behavior) has steadily become more convincing; and even chimp morality is persuasively defended. Dolphins, too, exhibit self-awareness, as well as other less intelligent animals. So Elizabeth's mentality does not necessarily estrange her from the natural world – not strictly. In fact, her mental gifts and their manifestations appear only to be more highly developed examples of natural equivalents. We can say then that Elizabeth's mentality is a uniqueness of *degree* more than of kind, which parallels how her physicality is a uniqueness of *expression* more than of kind. Though Elizabeth can perform mental feats that seem to us extremely un-animal, still, even while wielding these astonishing talents, she remains embedded within the continuum of nature.

Difference of Kind

Now though let us examine where Elizabeth steps aside, where, as she stands sweating and making obligatory eye contact with her classmates, endeavoring to shape her future, hoping to excel in her speech and determined to graduate and commence a satisfying independence, she transcends the natural world.

All animals, including human beings, engage their environments with the same intentions. Every species exploits its surroundings for the continuation of its own existence, extracting sustenance from it and security. The difference between how an African lion goes about doing this, however, and how Elizabeth does so is marked -- They traverse their worlds in very different moods. Daily the lion contends with challenges both subtle and savage to assure his survival. But once he feels replenished and safe he stops. The lion hunts and feeds. He waters. He nests and mates. He sleeps. The lion contends with his environment until his needs are met and then he rests. Elizabeth and the rest of us, on the other hand, do not merely contend with our environment to ensure our existence for today, tomorrow, or next week. Look at where Elizabeth stands, for instance. Already she has fed and watered like that African lion, and yet still she feels compelled to anxiously deliver this presentation to her class. She stands there hoping for a sufficient grade. She stands intending to graduate in a few weeks. She stands aiming for some unchosen occupation that she hopes will sustain her through her adulthood. Elizabeth seeks to control her environment more forcefully, in other words, to dominate it comprehensively in order to guarantee her existence for a longer period of time. We can roughly say then that wild animals move in a mood of *Contention* as they exploit their environment, while human beings move in a more forceful mood of *Domination*.

While Elizabeth's biology is a uniqueness of expression more than kind, and Elizabeth's mentality is a uniqueness of degree more than kind, this mood Elizabeth moves in while exploiting her environment is most decidedly a difference of kind. Wild animals do not seek to dominate their environment. They may contend with it, engage it fiercely, even savagely kill competing beings in it to assure their own survival, but once their survival seems assured they rest. Human beings are not satisfied with just surviving. Humans manhandle their surroundings, reshape them not only toward survival but also according to their desires and whims, and abstract fears. So while human biology and human mentality keep Elizabeth within the continuum of nature, it is how Elizabeth employs these to exploit her environment where she transcends that continuum. It is her mood of Domination. This point is fundamental to our investigation: For this disconnection from the natural, and how it conflicts with what remains natural in Elizabeth's physicality and mentality, is the ultimate source of our feeling of emptiness.

What is Domination?

Before I go on to present the implications of this assertion, it is worth spending a few sentences trying to convey more exactly the difference between the wild animal's mood of Contention and the modern human's mood of Domination.

Here are some illustrations:

A puma stalks, kills, and eats a wild deer. This is Contention. A human being traps a wild deer and from it breeds tame deer which he can kill and eat at his convenience. This is Domination.

A troop of chimpanzees patrols and guards a piece of territory to defend the

[34]

sustenance gained from its hunting and gathering grounds. This is Contention. A tribe of humans patrols and guards a piece of territory to defend its sustenance; but once that area is secured, it seeks then to expand that territory to include grounds it could never exploit solely by itself. This is Domination.

A black bear occupies a cave through winter, but in spring abandons it. This is Contention. A human being occupies or constructs a dwelling, and then establishes a claim to it that guarantees her nearly irreversible possession over it for as long as she wills. This is Domination.

A generalized definition of the wild animal's mood of Contention then would be that wild animals feel compelled to seek and take from the environment what they require for their immediate and near-term needs. While a generalized definition of the human mood of Domination would be that homo sapiens feel compelled to transform their environment with a view toward assuring the provision of their needs for an extended, even limitless, time.

A surer understanding of what I mean by these two dissimilar compulsions, however, is better intuited from their less exact *moods* instead of from more objective definitions.

In Contention, one interacts with the present, with the now, spending the bulk of one's hours living one's life instead of projecting, planning, and toiling. One eats one's acquired food. One sleeps. One roams. One mates. This is how wild animals live. Wild animals exist mostly in the current moment of being. As a result, a wholeness imbues their world and psyche. An unbrokenness. A continuity. They may be in conflict with their environment, but they are not in opposition to it. They are integrated with their environment.

[37]

When one lives in the mood of Domination, however, only rarely does one live in the present moment. Chiefly one lives to protect oneself from the uncertainties of the next moment, to conquer the next moment; and one does so by continually considering past moments, by applying knowledge gained from prior experience. Most meaningful to the mood of Domination, therefore, is conquest (the future), and applying the lessons of experience (the past). Psychologically, very little of the mood of Domination springs from the current moment of being. This prohibits humans from integrating wholly with our envi-

ronment. It situates us in direct opposition to our environment. In fact,
constantly we wrangle it, confront it,
struggle to subdue it.

As Elizabeth presents her informative
report she has a strategic vision of how it
and her other studious efforts will profit
her many years from today. That vision
may not be exactly precise, but she
presumes that by consciously weaving
together her world and her emerging
talents, and deliberately steering these
toward some general purpose, she will
eventually reap some sustaining benefits.
This is about the future. This is

Domination. The infant chimpanzee observes his mother fishing grubs from a stump with a stick simply because that infant chimp happens to be riding his mother's back at that moment. Later, as a juvenile or adult, he will notice grubs in a stump and fish them out with a stick to eat them. Both in the acquisition of that learned technique and in his later application of that technique the chimp lives primarily in his current moment of being. He lives in the present. He lives in a mood of Contention.

In none of the species left to their natural habitats do we find human-style anxieties or suicides or culturally-induced psychoses. We witness none of the wild animals fretting compulsively, from minute to minute, about potentialities over which they have no immediate awareness or direct control. The nearest we come to seeing Elizabeth's mental discomfort with emptiness in the animal kingdom is among the animals we hold captive or which we have domesticated. And in these we can recognize the rudiments of our own Dominating psychology. Elizabeth's cat Captain learns her routines and impetuously signals her when his feeding time arrives, Dominating to a degree both her and his larger environment. As he Dominates we see also in Captain how Elizabeth's delays or denials of his desire frustrate him, raking him with anxiety. Even with a modicum of Domination as miniscule as this, Captain and our other domestic pets appear to join us in our psychic tension, fretting in patterns that recall ours, and becoming susceptible, according to animal behaviorists, to human-like psychoses.

If we survey all the species of the natural world we see that we and our domesticated and captive animals are the only sentient beings on planet Earth that suffer this brand of anxiety. When reacting to our emptiness on a daily basis, we can readily identify a myriad of potential sources and cues and triggers that prick its discomfort, like say the fear of delivering a public address, or the irritations of freeway navigation. There are numberless culprits upon which to lay blame. But by comparing the whole of our single species to the millions of wild ones on the planet, we can, rather guardedly at this point, pin the source of our emptiness on exactly one culprit. For if the principal trait that separates us from the wild animals is how we relate to the environment, or, in other words, our mood of Domination, then perhaps that trait is also what distances us from them psychologically.

At this stage such an assertion seems overbroad and flimsy. But if we examine the origins and evolution of Domination, the correlation becomes more tantalizing. For we can trace the behavior of wild animals and homo sapiens backward in time and describe both when our modern mood of Domination diverged from their natural mood of Contention and what that transition looked like. Dissecting the emergence and growth of Domination in our species exposes its integral components and overarching structure. And a knowledge of these greatly illuminates the emptiness within us.

part two

Toward Human

Our forebears did not always move through their environment wielding this mood of Domination. Humanity's ancestors were once wild animals in every sense of the term. Before 10 million years ago (to be conservative) our ancestors had not yet evolved away from the common ancestor we share with the chimpanzees. Therefore, before 10 million years ago our ancestors and the ancestors of chimpanzees were one and the same species. At that point we were categorically a wild animal and moving in the wild animal's mood of Contention.

After 10 million years ago our hereditary line began to distinguish itself from this common ancestor. By 3.6 million years ago our mode of locomotion had diverged from that of other primates decidedly. Instead of knuckle-walking across the forest floor or the savannah, a forebear of Elizabeth, let's call her *E*, started to walk upright on two feet. This was a defining change in our evolutionary line. Was it then that *E* became human as we think of human beings today? Was it then that *E* began to Dominate? Is this all it took? To walk upright? Archeological evidence, or its lack, shows that through those first millions of years the mood of our ancestors' behavior paralleled that of other primates. Walking upright did not alter this. We simply became a bipedal primate. *E*, thus, interacted with her surroundings just as wild animals do now -- through the mood of Contention.

This stasis of behavior began to change 2.6 million years ago. About then *E* started to fashion crude tools. Her first set of tools were simple hammerstones, scrapers, choppers, and sharp flakes that she made by striking one rock against another. Analyses of surface wear on these implements tell us they cut, chopped, scraped, and severed plants and butchered animals. Her second set of tools, which emerged about 1.7 million years ago, was more advanced. Now, instead of just crudely bashing stones against each other to create a useful edge or some keen flakes, *E* began to impose preconceived shapes onto her material using a mental template to guide her manufacture. Tools echoing the earlier kit persisted but were joined now by more impressive hand axes, cleavers, and picks. These were used for cutting, digging, skinning, and to cut plants and wood and to butcher animals. About 315,000 years ago *E* refined her tool kit yet again. By then some of the mental templates she followed were so sophisticated that she could not fashion the tools in a single stage of work. *E* first carefully shaped a

[*52*]

stone core; then she struck from that core the envisioned tool. This new level of preparation complicated her manufacture considerably, which reflected a notable advance in E's mental capabilities and culture. But still her tools cut wood, butchered animals, and processed skins.

As each level of sophistication broadened the gamut and effectiveness of E's tool kit, and as E began to husband fire in basic ways, she grew more and more exceptional among the wild animals surrounding her -- not just culturally, but also physically. By the time of the first tool kit her brain size had expanded from the 400 cc chimp-size brain to a 600 cc brain.

By the second tool kit it had jumped from the 600 cc brain to a 900 cc brain. And by the third tool kit it had enlarged from the 900 cc brain to a 1200 cc brain. Physically, E's brain size increased synchronously with the greater complexity of her tool kits, edging ever closer to our 1400 cc volume. And culturally, as her tools demonstrate, E had progressed well beyond other wild animals. So is this when E became a human as we conceive of human beings today? As soon as she started making tools and growing her cultural footprint and intelligence did she supplant the wild animal's mood of

Contention with our mood of Domination?

The brevity with which I outline this evolution belies the time it took for it to transpire. Two million years it took to progress from bashing one rock against another to produce a tool to shaping a rock into a prescribed form so it could be bashed to produce a tool. And though the archeological evidence surrounding these tool kits details a creeping advance in production techniques and finished results, along with corresponding shifts in behavior – like the consumption of new foods – it does not reveal detectable changes in the psychological mood of the individuals employing them. The later tools were used to cut plants and to butcher animals, just as the earliest of them were used to cut plants and to butcher animals. The tools of these cultures do not suggest a mood of Domination. They do not equip *E* to *control* her environment but help her more to *survive* in it as always she had. So, regardless their admirable growth in sophistication, and the proof they provide of *E*'s burgeoning intelligence, these tool cultures indicate an improving struggle to stay equal with nature, not a means of mastering it.

Tools and culture, moreover, do not fundamentally estrange homo sapiens from the natural world. Roughly one percent of all animals, across nine different classes, employ tools in some way. Chimpanzees wield sticks to harvest grubs, as mentioned; but also they use leaves as sponges and stones to crack nuts. In fact, tool cultures vary across different troops of wild chimpanzees in Africa regarding which implements serve what purpose and exactly how they are finessed. What E accomplished with her tool kits differs only in degree from what wild animals are observed to accomplish today. Culture and the wild animal's mood of Contention can coexist. Culture does not require the mood of Domination.

In sum, through these millions of years our forebears evolved toward us in brain size and rudimentary culture; and we see proof of their expanding intelligence. But there is no evidence yet to suggest they moved in a mood different from that of the wild animals neighboring them. *E* was an intelligent wild animal adept at manufacturing tools, but immersed still in the mood that governed the wilderness surrounding her, she used those tools to Contend with her environment, not to Dominate it.

The Early Humans

Even at about 100,000 years ago, as our ancestors acquired essentially the human brain case as we know it today, this mood of Contention continued. A cultural spareness stretching from our earliest forebears and through this preliminary stage of modern humans shows this. At 100,000 years ago anatomically modern homo sapiens did not live in a psychological mood appreciably distinct from those of our ancestors who produced the tool kits of 315,000 years ago, or those who chipped into existence the hand axes of 1.7 million years ago, or

[59]

those who bashed apart the choppers and scrapers of 2.6 million years ago, or even those just beginning to walk upright 3.6 million years ago. According to the artifacts these human beings left behind, nothing about their psychological approach to life substantially changed after they crossed that final threshold into physically modern humanity.

Remarkable in this regard are anatomical studies that conclude the E of 100,000 years ago to be virtually our duplicate physically. So much so that we should now give her a new name. We will evolve her from E to Liza. Liza had all of our physical characteristics. She had the same brain size, body type, stride, and elegance as her descendent Elizabeth who will deliver an oral presentation in a classroom 100,000 years later. Passing Liza on a sidewalk today we would not note her as unusual. And natural selection would demand that if she had the anatomical structures to make speech possible (which she did with her lowered pharynx and parabolic-shaped mouth), and a thought capacity deep enough to drive language (which she did with a brain size and configuration matching ours), that the voicings she used to communicate before entering anatomical modernity would evolve almost immediately into language. More exact articulation would be selected for heavily by evolution due to the greater cooperation and insight it would allow this social being in her struggle for a livelihood. As soon as language was possible, in other words, Liza would begin to speak. It is quite possible, in fact, our ancestors were speaking well before they became fully modern.

So this modern human being, Liza, was just like us in two ways: Bodily she was our mirror image -- you would not remark her on the street. Intellectually she was our equal -- you could converse with her if you spoke her tongue. But psychologically, according to the evidence she left, still she dwelled in another mood, in the mood of Contention, in the mood of the wild animal. Even as she became a physically modern human, as modern biologically as our nervously perspiring Elizabeth and her politely attentive classmates, Liza still moved in that mood of Contention; still she related to the environment the way a wild chimpanzee does, fighting it for survival, wresting from it what she required for the near-term, living more or less in the present moment.

The Advent of Domination

Around 50,000 years ago something happened. Whether the event is isolated and fixed on the timeline of our evolution is vigorously debated, and in the 250,000 years previous to the event other comparable advances may have made false starts and petered out. But, in general, when referring to the populations that would seed our contemporary society, by about 50,000 years ago the relationship of human beings with their environment had changed. Suddenly they no longer moved in the mood of the wild animals. Suddenly they no longer just Contended for a livelihood and shelter, satisfied to occupy the present moment. Suddenly homo sapiens began to Dominate. It's like an explosion. Artifacts and behaviors never before seen erupt across human culture. Suddenly humans innovate a vast new array of tools. Suddenly humans are accessing many more raw materials in the fabrication of those tools. Suddenly humans produce their tools following more formalized and structured patterns. Suddenly humans are gathering a wider variety of plants. Suddenly humans are hunting a wider variety of game. Suddenly human hunting strategies become so effective that human-made animal extinctions occur. Humans are suddenly engineering more elaborate architectures. They are suddenly carrying about the first pieces of portable art. They are migrating into climes previously lethal to them -- and making fire now as they go instead of just husbanding it. Suddenly they are trading with one another, and communicating over greater distances, and becoming more complex socially, and even diverging culturally. All of this in an archeological eye blink. Of a sudden. None of these cultural traits are observed across the whole of the human species before this period. Ever. This sudden outburst of creativity, in fact, ends eons of unimaginably slow technological and cultural progress. Over the tens of thousands of generations preceding this period, humans had abided a pattern of culture without substantial change. For tens of thousands of generations! And then, suddenly, in less than some two thousand generations everything shifted. The force of human intelligence and industry erupts onto the archeological record. Evidence of their application is identifiable across the spectrum of human artifacts. Homo sapiens no longer bash only rocks into tools, but acquire and work flint and bone and antler and ivory. They no longer scavenge or down the more vulnerable individuals of a herd, but craft bows and arrows and spear-throwers toward more robust and dangerous prey. And some desert now their thatch and mud huts for more complicated dwellings of stone. And instead of merely sheltering in caves occasionally, they commence to express their anxieties or passions or resolve their spiritual or social conflicts across cave walls. Each of these behaviors is novel and illuminates the human being's new relationship with her world. And that relationship is one of *control*. Suddenly, what had been a Contention with the environment, a mere surviving of it, a breathtaking battle for equality with it, a teetering equilibrium with it, becomes a control of the environment, a Domination of it. This sudden shift in psychology, this seismic break from a mindset rooted even in the earliest lifeforms of Earth, is human beings falling out of their original relationship with the world, humans de-integrating themselves from that precarious balance, humans beginning to take possession of their environment and future. After 250,000 years of probably stumbling into the mood of Domination, and then losing it again, and then discovering it again, and then losing it again, at last human populations congealed enough demographically to allow this highly effective perspective to propagate across bands and tribes when it emerged a final time. Following that, humans as a species no longer moved in a mood of Contention like their animal brethren. They no longer were limited to a life of tenuous survival. Something more they craved now, and sought. So it was here that Liza took her most significant step toward becoming Elizabeth.

Eden and The Fall

Prior to this creative explosion human beings traversed their world with the same outlook as wild animals, in Contention; after it, they Dominated. This extraordinary pivot yields two points of interest for this investigation into our emptiness: One, it signals to us the birth of the psychologically modern human being, a being different enough now from her earlier incarnations that she requires a new name -- call her Beth; and, two, it injects a profound implication into the 50,000 years or more before this sudden or gradual change. For our purpose, for the purpose of thoroughly comprehending our emptiness, the most enlightening implication we can glean from this transformation is that *once humans just like us lived without Dominating their environment.* For the 50,000 years or more before this monumental shift they lived as modern humans just like us, introspective beings with all our mental faculties -- thinking abstractly, formulating strategies, using language -- but instead of exercising these capacities to impose a mood of Domination, they exercised them through a mood of Contention. During that epoch our ancestors existed more in the spirit of wild animals than modern

[72]

humans; though simultaneously they enjoyed every talent and power of the modern human mind. This change to a mood of Domination, and the fact an extended period preceded it during which a strikingly different mood governed our behavior, demonstrates that the Domination that defines us today is not the only relationship with our surroundings we have lived by as modern human beings. The mood of Domination seems our only possible mode of existence because our rearing teaches us no other. But, according to the descriptions elucidated here, we do not *have* to Dominate. In fact, for at least half our history as anatomically modern humans we did *not* Dominate.

The mood of Domination *is* natural to us in the sense that it was probable for us. The competitive advantages of Domination lie latent in Liza, and an awakening and developing of those advantages would improve her chances of survival. It was probable then that natural selection would tease the capabilities forth eventually and reshape Liza into Beth. In this way the mood of Domination is natural. But across the millions upon millions of years preceding Domination's advent our psychology evolved to Contend with our surroundings, not to Dominate them. So our psyches today are predisposed to Contend. We are still born to Contend. Children still Contend in their early years. And even as adults, as we Dominate, often we long to escape the burdensomeness of the mood. But our minds are prodded and channeled into Domination continually, conditioned every day, nearly every minute. So we have not yet assimilated this psychological shift of some 50,000 years ago. We have not yet reconciled our psyche born to be in balance with the environment and integrated into it with our relatively new perspective which compels us to control it.

Today, in order to survive, we have to Dominate. But since our original psychology -- a psychology with which we are all still born – feels unnatural Dominating, constantly we live in ways that feel disconsonant to us, that disturb our inner coherence and integrity. Within ourselves, therefore, ceaselessly we resist how we live. This creates knots inside us -- knots of discontent, of dissatisfaction, of discomfort, of unease, of imbalance. We are at odds with ourselves. This is what births the rift we feel: That to survive in our society, we have to split our being: We have to sense our natural inclinations of Contention, but then sacrifice those natural inclinations to the unnatural demands of Domination. On those late nights, or lonely Sundays, or random moments on her sofa when suddenly Elizabeth feels haunted by her emptiness and hurts what she is feeling is this split, this rift, this inner contradiction. When she yearns for a wholeness, she is yearning for the undivided wholeness of the mood of Contention; she is yearning for the coherence and harmony of her original psychology.

Elizabeth's Challenge

When Elizabeth woke this morning she drew open her curtains to view the golden luster of the warming April trees. After the long frigid winter she craved a stroll. Elizabeth wanted to slide into her favorite knit cap, slice and salt a crisp red apple to carry along, and just go for a walk. But she feared that skipping her speech class might stall her graduation, which would put at risk the IT jobs she has applied for, which would jeopardize the tentative career trajectory she envisions for herself, which would be a rather inauspicious start for her coming independence. So, reluctantly, instead of munching that fresh apple and enjoying that sunny stroll, Elizabeth showered, donned her plain khakis and black polo shirt, mounted the freeway, arrived at her classroom, and delivered her dreaded presentation. Elizabeth dismissed her natural inclinations and acceded to society's requirements. Elizabeth quashed her longing to Contend, and she Dominated.

Given the descriptions adduced thus far, it might seem the easiest way for Elizabeth to reclaim a feeling of wholeness, to seal that rift within herself and return to an inner completeness, would be to simply stroll out into that golden April and enjoy those crisp wedges of apple, or, in other words, to stop Dominating and start again Contending. While theoretically this is true, the realities of our human society complicate such a direct and immediate response. For though the mood of Domination emerged in us as human individuals, and matured and proliferated across human communities, at this point in our evolution human beings no longer totally control it. Domination has acquired a life of its own. This fact superimposes onto our emptiness and its pain an additional dimension,

and it is a dimension very difficult for us
to escape.

part three

Domination Squared

As we live now, in our modern society, every human being has to interact with our mood of Domination on two levels. First, inwardly, by wrestling with the inner conflicts and unease it sows within us as just described. But also outwardly. For at this stage in our evolution our mood of Domination has transcended all of us as individuals to become a collective external phenomenon.

Left alone, Elizabeth could return to her original psychology, to the mood of Contention. She could live in the present moment and take that morning walk and munch that enticing apple. But Elizabeth cannot survive by herself. She can only maintain her life and health by participating in our human society. And human society will not allow her to merely Contend with her environment. In fact, in return for that picturesque lane she craves to stroll and that apple she might slice (or, in return for the shelter and nourishment, and clothing that human society provides Elizabeth), it *demands* that she and the rest of us Dominate. For it is by Dominating the environment that we produce these goods and services. The rub here is that Elizabeth too is a part of the environment. So, in order to produce the goods and services that assure our continued existence, we, as a society, also have to Dominate Elizabeth. If we are to engage our emptiness and its pain comprehensively, we have to internalize this point as frankly as we can: Just as we as individuals Dominate our environment, human society, which is our collective form, has come to Dominate *us* as a *part* of that environment.

This fact is the most significant stimulus to Elizabeth's and mine and your pain. For it compounds the hurt of our emptiness profoundly by distorting how we perceive it, how we interpret it, and how we react to it. Examining how this societal manifestation of our Domination evolved over time provides insights into how it warps our understanding now. And these insights better equip us to grapple with how our collective Domination exacerbates our pain.

The Shamans

When Liza Contended with the world, when Liza was equal to the world, in balance with it, like a wild animal, she was completely integrated with it. She clashed with her environment certainly as she struggled to exist, but, being intrinsic to that environment, Liza never moved in opposition to it. Even in her fiercest fights Liza remained an organic part of her surroundings and was governed by their natural laws. No one reading this essay can identify with Liza's state of mind. Our lack of this integration, our separateness from our environment, actually serves as the very foundation for how we perceive our world. In our current mode of being the world is different from us, alien. We live in opposition to it. Of the maiden expressions of this our modern human perspective, the most illuminating are found in ancient cave art dating from 60,000 to 12,000 years ago.

Theorists have advanced various meanings for the magnificent cave paintings of Europe and Indonesia and elsewhere. In the early days of research it was proposed the paintings were meant as hunting magic, like talismans, to bring game under human influence and guarantee or swell the bounty of the hunt. More recently and with more persuasive profundity the paintings have been argued as elements of initiation rights and social organization. But, regardless their literal intentions, one conclusion is unavoidable: Because the cave paintings could not have been created before the mood of Domination came to human beings, they must, at their most fundamental level, convey a reaction to the mood of Domination itself. Either consciously or unconsciously, the masters of these artworks addressed the human soul falling out of balance with the natural world and acquiring our modern Dominating psychology.

The paintings plainly reveal that Beth had awakened in a new way to the elements around her, and to her discreteness from them. No longer was she embedded in the seamless mind of the natural world like Liza or *E*, or like today's wild animals. If she were, she could not have fashioned the images in the first place. In the very act of portraying a bison, an auroch, or a horse, indirectly Beth made her separation from them her subject matter. And she portrayed this separation because she felt a need to understand it. Through these paintings, Beth was trying to comprehend what had happened to her soul. Like the art we create today, ultimately those super-ancient paintings attempted to repair or describe a wholeness that had been broken, a wholeness that Beth had lost. Already, even that early, those newly psychologically modern human beings yearned and sought and struggled to participate again fully in the unbroken wholeness of the natural environment surrounding them; the wholeness they could sense, just as we can, but which they had lost, just as we have. With these early artworks they were seeking to reclaim that wholeness for themselves, just as each of us still do.

Eventually these initial wrestlings with our emptiness would spawn spiritual beliefs. For as humans fell out of the wholeness of their original psychology inevitably two proto-spiritual phenomena would occur: One, an image or an idea would emerge from their broken souls that symbolized the wholeness they had lost; and, two, those special few persons who could help humans to heal their emptiness and touch again that original wholeness would be recognized and sought out. Here was the birth of a great spirit, or divinity, and alongside it, the birth of shaman. Suggestions of these appear in that super-ancient art.

Most significant to our investigation into the pain of our emptiness, though, is that, ironically, even in these first sallies to reclaim our original wholeness through art, humans were constructing a new kind of psychological environment for themselves. These paintings and the spiritualities and cultures that developed around them created an environment for

[94]

people of their *own* making. It was a human environment now through which each mind had to move consciously, a human environment to which each mind had to react. So this environment, as a human creation, established a new degree of separation between Beth and her original wild-animal state. It became a norm outside of Beth by which Beth had to judge herself, a norm other than her own natural being against which to compare her actions and urges, and desires. She now moved consciously aware that she was part of a human structure into which she fit and by which she would be valued. She now had a human psychological construct above and around her, guiding her; a human ideal that directed her and limited her. In its mere existence, therefore, human spiritual culture began conditioning Beth farther and farther away from her original psychology. It skewed Beth's natural comprehension of her surrounding world, giving its components new meanings, *societal* meanings. As a result, human spiritual culture curtailed the borderless psychological freedom Beth once enjoyed in experiencing her own existence and her world.

In the cave paintings and other early forms of art we see our mood of Domination broaden into a collective manifestation. Our Domination transcended humans as individuals during this period to become a phenomenon shared and experienced by numbers of humans in a communal way. Not only did we now Dominate personally, but the melding of our individual Dominating moods transformed kinship networks into the first Dominating societies. Beth's children grew up in a culture where everything human around them -- from the clothes they wore, to the words they spoke, to how they acquired food -- was an expression of Domination, and so, automatically, infused them with the mood of Domination. Her children would rarely know a different psychology. Rarely would they be exposed to any relationship with the environment other than Domination. Like us, they would rarely then in their adult minds even become aware of the mood of Contention. And almost never as adults would they experience the integrated wholeness that originally birthed them. Once this social evolution had fully matured, in fact, every human being born from that time forward would be trained into the mood of Domination without knowing it. Irresistibly every human soul became destined to the same pain of emptiness that you and I and Elizabeth feel.

The Priests

Yet, during the many millennia of the cave painting cultures Beth still enjoyed *indirect* access to the wholeness of nature. The new human environment she helped to populate blocked her from participating in that wholeness, but the human environment itself maintained a mindful connection with the natural world. We see this in the paintings themselves. The images demonstrate the importance of untamed nature to those early societies, unequivocally showing how the beasts of the wild still weighed heavily upon human consciousness. So while Beth was estranged from that natural wholeness, still she sensed its nearness, and keenly. And with the intervention of a shaman, as the cave portrayals suggest, she could sometimes break through her mood of Domination, return to her original psychology, and temporarily taste her original wholeness.

Beginning about 12,000 years ago this final culture-wide nexus with the natural world evaporated. Before this turning point Beth and her cohorts moved with and among wild animals as they hunted

[100]

them. Beth also mingled through the flora of her environment as she foraged plant foods. So at least while acquiring their sustenance Beth and friends experienced an intimacy with their natural surr-oundings. When humans began to favor and cultivate select plants, however, and capture and herd select animals to the point of domestication this final intimacy faded. Agriculture and animal husbandry, and the organization it took to produce, process, and distribute their products, demanded a much more Dominating type of society. And to affect this Domination required a more exacting political and religious structure. As these societal structures adapted to the intricacies of a domestication economy they removed themselves, at different times in different places over thousands of years, farther and farther from the natural world. Eventually humans did not interact with the wholeness of nature to acquire their sustenance. At all. A day came that entire cultures, cultures like ours, inhabited their own human-made environments exclusively, for every activity, rarely relating to the natural world surrounding them. In other words, about 12,000 years ago, with the advent of agriculture and pastoralism, the early human Dominating cultures of the cave painters began evolving into society as we experience it today. The hunt became the grain house and the herd. The shaman became the priest. And the distance between Beth's quotidian psychology and her original psychology arrived at a gap recognizable to us. Society completely overwhelmed the individual. We entered into history as we know it.

The impact of this change upon our emptiness is staggering. Instead of Beth being naturally integrated with the wholeness of nature like *E* or Liza, or having a shaman to help her break through her perceptions of separation, during this agricultural evolution Beth was taught that no independent path toward wholeness existed for her; that there was no personal path to inner peace. Priests now taught Beth that the potent mystic yearnings she felt within her breast could only be assuaged by obedience to the deities of her culture. Only by the grace of those gods, she learned, could her emptiness be replenished, could she be reconciled with the completeness she sensed and thirsted after. Beth's spiritual quest became dictated totally now by the culture into which she was indoctrinated, by the lessons her society drummed into her. Her search was governed by the "truths" of her culture, and by the fact those "truths" blinded her to or barred her from the inborn freedom she owned as a human being to pursue and reclaim her original wholeness by herself. Only by her culture could Beth be saved now. And she had to abide by this. For if Beth did not, she would starve. Here was the final and densest barrier our mood of Domination would erect between us and our original wholeness, and so the deepest sting to our emptiness. Our mood of Domination came now to control how we defined, interpreted, and wrestled with our own inner pain. It had tamed and subjugated our spiritual quest. In doing so Domination finally severed us completely from our natural origins, divorcing us almost irretrievably from our original relationship with the environment and the wholeness of our original psychology. Human society Dominated now our souls.

What Beth felt psychologically, therefore, sometime amid the evolution of agriculture, differs little from what every living human feels today. She shared our mental turmoil and parried the same conflicts we do: One, an individual's instinctual sense of her lost wholeness and the urge to reclaim that wholeness. Two, an individual's need to preserve her existence by participating in the mood of

Domination. Three, how society distorts the individual's spiritual quest in a way to ensure the survival of society. And, four, how any attempt to solve one of these three problems contradicts the solution of the other two. This psychological conundrum became the problem of every individual human being. Just as it is still a conundrum for every individual human being. So it was here that Beth became just like us. It was here that Beth became Elizabeth.

Our Collective Quandary

Our quandary of Domination is a compound phenomenon. Not only do we carry the raw problem of the mood of Domination within us personally, which warps us away from our predisposition to Contend with the environment, and divides us within; but we imbibe Domination passively, unconsciously, through the cultural forms it has assumed; and actively, too, as its collective form *teaches* us to Dominate, and even *requires we Dominate* in order to survive. Further, due to the cultural parameters we absorb through instruction and emulation, *we seem to have no choice* but to Dominate.

At our very birth society begins grooming us to Dominate. And by the time we have matured enough to question the mood of Domination critically, to ponder whether it suits our individual needs, the mood so completely controls our worldview that we lack the mental independence necessary to counter it. We have not the words, the ideas, the merest foothold for critiquing our training at this profoundest level. No mechanism exists for us to challenge the foundation upon which our own persona stands. Domination weaves itself so subtly and inextricably through our being that we fail to even question whether it be evil or good, productive or destructive, positive or negative. Its everpresence blinds us to its presence. It just *is*. Domination must be correct, we think, because that's all there is. There's no other way, we think. Yet, within us we *feel* the other way. This makes our rift unceasing. And this aggravates our pain immeasurably. *For it makes of our emptiness a mystery.* Something is wrong, we always feel. The sense nags us. It plagues us. It haunts us. Everything is wrong, we feel. But everything can't be wrong, we tell ourselves. Because everything is just as it has always been. There is no other way. But this perennial conclusion of ours only reflects the completeness of Domination's influence over our reasoning. For an alternate path does exist, obscured and forgotten though it may be. Modern human society just holds no place for it.

These ingredients are principal to the pain of our emptiness: This confusion, this feeling of helplessness before an elusive mystery, this sense of a wrongness we cannot quite name or articulate. But these discontents arise from the fact we are trained to contradict our own nature; and from how vigorously and thoroughly our society then enforces this self-contradiction, blinding us even to the existence of an alternative form of behavior. But an alternative does exist. We *can* interact with the world more naturally, in a manner that harmonizes our personalities with our original nature. Just recognizing this possibility reduces our helplessness and confusion, which eases our pain. Human beings are born to Contend not to Dominate. Comprehending this helps us hurt less.

part four

A Return to Contention

So how do we return to this mood of Contention? This is the persisting question for anyone who has read this far. How do we heal that rift of emptiness, step back into the present moment, reclaim our original psychology and its natural wholeness? The answer is embedded in how Domination evolved within the human psyche in the first place. And this is best illustrated through how animals and human beings process one of life's most salient elements: Death.

In the natural world, in the world of Contention, as far as researchers can determine, individuals relate to death instinctually and reactively. Studies observing how the most intelligent of our animal relatives engage with the phenomenon of death suggest they do not wrestle with it abstractly like humans. They demonstrate a fear of and flight instinct from stimuli understood to threaten death, which we share. And some species apparently grieve death once individuals close to them succumb. But animals seem not to *prepare* for death psychologically, or *dread* it like human beings. In the modern human world, on the other hand, an abstract awareness of death and preparation and prevention of death could be considered a primary motivator for much of our activity.

Humans think about death abstractly and seriously all the time.

Examining the transition from a more reactive appreciation of death, which animals demonstrate, to a more deliberative appreciation of death, which modern humans demonstrate, will help us not only understand how the human faculties evolved into the mood of Domination but also how we can silence the mood of Domination.

The Role of Death

Around 100,000 years ago when Liza became anatomically modern like us (and probably before), she began to process the coming and passage of death as emotionally and profoundly as we do. Liza comprehended the gravity of death and feared its arrival, and when it took her loved ones she mourned their passing. But in that first 50,000 years or more, before her faculties had fully distilled the mood of Domination, she saw no alternate reaction to death beyond her passive submission to it and grief. Death was like a thunderstorm. Liza could see it coming, and cower beneath its ominous hovering, and worry about its awesome downpour, but she would not try to stop it. Resisting death was as futile as resisting the rain. It would not even occur to her to try. This was the mind of homo sapiens in transition from the mood of Contention to the mood of Domination. Liza understood death the way modern humans do, but she still reacted to death the way the natural world does. Liza dreaded and wept over death like us, but she did not yet attempt to control it like us. No longer innocent and indifferent like the wild animals, but not yet able to resist it as we do, Liza moved in a mentality that both completely appreciated the meaning of death but was also fatefully resigned to it. This may sound alien to us, hardly possible, but it is a necessary bridge mentality from that of animal psychology to modern human psychology. And such a psychological limbo must have occurred -- For once we were wild animals.

But then Liza became Beth.

For as Liza began to discover the technologies of Domination, and with them haphazardly shape her environment in more forceful ways, by extension she began to counter the possibility of death in more forceful ways. To do one was to do the other. Liza did not one day pronounce: "I will now seek to prevent my death." Instead, as her mood of Domination began to control her surr-oundings, she began concurrently to minimize the variables that could cause her death, but also to maximize the variables that could prolong her life. In doing so Liza began situating death in opposition to herself, just as she did nature. Gradually, as she transformed into the Beth of that momentous creative shift of about 50,000 years ago, death no longer towered over her, hunted her, and addled her, like an unmanageable element, like a thunderstorm; it became now a possibility more removed, a phenomenon Beth could consider separate from her environs, one she could even resist. So as homo sapiens eased into opposition with their world, simultaneously they came into opposition with death.

Our gateway out of our mood of Domination is found right here: In the fact that our appreciation of death was entangled with, or even undergirded, the evolutionary mechanisms that drew us into the mood of Domination. It is how we relate to death *now* that keeps Domination active in us. What else but our own hidden fears of death drive us to thoroughly Dominate the environment around us? Even many seemingly peripheral concerns of ours, if one digs out their originating impetuses, arise from a fear of losing one's livelihood, or of losing one's shelter, or perhaps a fear of losing a relation upon whom one depends, or with whom one identifies. All of these concerns, ultimately, have a bearing upon our continued existence, upon our death. If we assess honestly the motivations driving our Domination, we find embedded in them, deeply, a fear of death.

So how does this work?

Our fear of death spurs us to Dominate. Domination, in turn, creates the rift within us, which we feel as emptiness. Our emptiness then causes us pain, which awakens again our fear of death. We react then to our newly excited fear of death by

Dominating even more. This reinforces the rift within us, sustaining or even heightening our emptiness. And so again our emptiness triggers our fear of death. And on. And on.

The circularity of our fear of death triggering our mood of Domination which cultivates then the pain of our emptiness which leads again to our fear of death may be maddening, but such a cycle of stimulus and response has an inherent weakness that provides us our avenue of escape: We need only short-circuit the cycle. Perhaps we cannot, by will, simply switch off our mood of Domination, but certainly by will we can confront our fear of death, or confront the pain of our emptiness. And as soon as we stop fleeing our fear of death; as soon as we truly accept our inevitable demise, we cease to Dominate. Or, as soon as we embrace our emptiness, refusing to hide from its pain, we cease to Dominate. With either of these two acts we short-circuit the cycle. The self-perpetuation of Domination which begets emptiness which begets fear of death which begets Domination which begets emptiness is interrupted, however briefly. During that interruption we slip into the present moment and experience a semblance of the mood of Contention.

So this is our deliverance in a single sentence: In order to escape the mood of Domination we need only face our fear of death, or embrace the pain of our emptiness.

An Example

Such a mindset is difficult but not impossible. Take Elizabeth as an example. When she awakens on that April morning to gaze through the glowing window pane and desire a refreshing stroll -- with maybe that crisp red apple to bring along -- she has these mental barriers to overcome before carrying out her whim, each

[126]

of which is rooted in the mood of Domination: She has the dissatisfaction of her instructor to face. She has potentially the disapproval of her peers awaiting her, or even their scorn. She has to entertain the possibility that she might fail the speech class. And if she fails perhaps she will not complete her degree. And if she abandons school early perhaps she will never own a home or live a long life. In fact, as Elizabeth stands gazing pensively through that sunlit window, she may even foresee herself starving to death in her old age, or freezing to death under some freeway bridge. Each of these potential consequences drift through Elizabeth as she muses, subconsciously propping up her commitment to go through with her speech. They are examples of how our fear of death (intermixed oftentimes with fears of failure or ostracism) conspires to guide everything we do; how it creates a premonition that if we behave other than how we are directed to behave by our mood of Domination, we will likely destroy the life apparatus that keeps our persons alive and secure. This premonition insists that to ignore the guidance of our mood of Domination must certainly render us irredeemably vulnerable, completely at the mercy of fate, and, ultimately, in the presence of death itself.

So to assume this mindset, to short-circuit the cycle fueling her mood of Domination and actually take that simple but rebellious April walk, Elizabeth has to genuinely accept all these dire possibilities, even embrace them. Instead of flinching at the possibility of a failing grade, she invites it. Instead of angling to prevent the sneering of her peers, she welcomes it. Instead of shrinking from a fear of failure, or of poverty, or of death, Elizabeth embraces these, accepting their potential occurrence. For as soon as she embraces her fear of death, Elizabeth no longer feels compelled to Dominate her environment in order to protect herself from death. The cycle is interrupted. Her compulsion to Dominate is neutralized. Automatically Elizabeth reconnects then with her natural self and the present moment, which closes that rift within her, which seals her emptiness and eliminates its pain. She is off then on her morning walk, munching away at her apple. By embracing these discomforts, in essence, Elizabeth embraces her own annihilation. In doing so she disables how society uses our fear of annihilation to coerce us into Dominating. If we can accept our own death, society cannot manipulate us by leveraging our fear of death. If we can embrace the pain of our emptiness, society cannot persuade us with its false promises to end that pain if only we will Dominate. Embracing the fear counteracts the fear. Embracing the pain stalls the pain. We slip then out of the mood of Domination and experience a relative wholeness.

The tactic feels foolish, for sure. It feels like a very courting of death, or of pain. And for this reason it is a troublesome attitude to maintain. But if we return again to the wise ones we see such an attitude is not foreign to human thought. In fact, enlightened figures have been advocating this approach for millennia, though using different vocabulary. Note that at the center of all the world's belief systems stands the concept of faith, or surrender, or acceptance, or submission. And what are these but an embracing by the human mind of its potential annihilation, a rejection of fear, a *complete forsaking of all control.*

The Prophets

And so finally we have returned to the wise ones. And we bring to them now the problem of our Domination from two directions. The first and more ephemeral challenge is simply to stay aware that society teaches us to Dominate, and stimulates us to Dominate, and constantly pressures us to Dominate, but that by embracing our emptiness or mortality we can defuse society's coercive sway. And the second challenge is to more deliberately and actively seek out our original mood of Contention. Appropriately, the teachings of all the world's spiritual traditions can be divided into two distinct impulses that mirror these two challenges. Usually the impulses are mixed together, but they can be teased apart. One impulse I call the protective; the other I call the proactive.

In what I'm calling the protective impulse the spiritual traditions offer guidance which, in its own way, exposes the mechanisms of Domination, apprising us of its incessant warping of us, and hounding of us. In the Yamas of Hinduism, for example, or the Ten Courses of Unwholesome Action outlined by Buddhism, or the Seven Deadly sins of Christianity we find encouragements to physical control over the senses, to mental control over the materialistic tendency, along with exhortations to restrain the ego, and to keep faithful to truth. These encouragements help us to identify and deflect away the most potent inducements of Domination. And this aids us in accepting our emptiness and short-circuiting its self-perpetuation. Every tradition conveys equivalent admonishments or protective warnings. And all the great teachers emphasize we cannot arrive at the wholeness they exampled except by recognizing such inner burdens and either avoiding them or excising them.

In what I call the proactive impulse the spiritual traditions provide more deliberate and active treks toward the wholeness the wise ones embodied. In the Niyamas of Hinduism, for example, or Islamic Sufism, or the effortless action of

Taoism we are offered paths that broaden our insight and illuminate fundamental truths. These chaperone the seeker through purity, contemplation, and into a resounding harmony with all. In other words, the proactive counselings woo one toward a more inclusive mode of being, toward a frame of mind nearer the innocents and the wild, or, toward the mood of Contention. Additionally, besides their explicit advice, the prophets also left behind their implicit examples. From the detachment of Siddhartha, to the 'Lamb of God,' to the ecstasies of Ramakrishna, we are shown repeatedly, through all of their stories, personalities

[136]

shorn to their most essential humanity. In them we see the human being in its original state, freed of emptiness, exercising the wholeness of our original psychology.

Certainly billions of words have been written on the many spiritual traditions of Earth and their messages so I refer the reader to other works to explore this idea more fully. While reading further it is necessary only to take from this essay its primary thrust: That we are pursuing an awareness and behavior that is more inclusive and integrated, more innocent, more natural, less Dominating, less controlling. Importantly, I believe further investigation can be "god-neutral." Approaching these systems and perusing their paths to our original psychology requires neither that we believe in a god, nor that we recognize any particular figure as such. Though, if the tendencies of the wise ones themselves are indicative, neither does such a belief prevent our reclaiming our original psychology. Also it is important to distinguish between the prophets themselves and the religions that grew up around them, as religion, by its nature, is a form of Domination.

As A Child

The mood of Domination is not a *part* of us -- it is *put upon* us. Humans are not born to the mood of Domination. Humans are not born to emptiness. Modern humans are born just like the humans of 100,000 years ago -- to the integration and wholeness of Contention. The healthy infant of today enters life with exactly the same psychological matrix as the healthy infant born 100,000 years ago. Left alone, they would -- all of us would -- grow into the unconditioned personalities of that super-ancient epoch. Modern children actually maintain this unconditioned point of view for an extended while. It takes many years and arduous effort on the part of parents and guardians and teachers to compel children to accept the mood of Domination and to obey its demands of our behavior. Before this transformation is finalized, the immediacy and spontaneity in youngsters, and their giddy liberty and borderless wonder inspire those of us already corralled by Domination. And the frank innocence of children, and their credulity and unwary trust alarm us with how vulnerable it leaves them to the Dominating world. But each of us once was there. When kids inspire us, we are moved by an openness

[*140*]

and spontaneity and freedom that we all once embodied when we too were young. In other words, we each remember our original psychology from our *own personal experience* -- from our childhood days before our training overwhelmed our psyches and drummed us, defenseless, into the mood of Domination. We know of our original psychology because we have *experienced* our original psychology. To reclaim that wholeness, we need only reclaim a state we already own, a state buried deep within us, one smothered beneath our conditioning.

Our original psychology waits within. Unceasingly, even in our very feelings of

[141]

emptiness, our original completeness reminds us of its residual presence, of its desperation to manifest itself, of its craving to flourish and make us whole again. The pain of our emptiness is a signal to us, a flare from the core of our beings. The pain of our emptiness is our original self not being expressed. Once that original psychology becomes manifest, naturally one is whole, and, naturally, the emptiness dissipates. Our emptiness is a beacon, therefore. By turning toward it, by contemplating the scorching fire it beams through us, by even embracing its wretched pain, we can follow our emptiness back to its ultimate source, back to our original wholeness.

The Original Elizabeth

But how did our original psychology manifest itself in a prehistoric adult? As mentioned earlier, our super-ancient ancestors left us some indirect indications of what such a state of mind may have felt like. I emphasize here the word 'indirect' and recognize that the portrait I am about to draw is necessarily flawed since it arises from my fully-Dominating mind attempting to extrapolate from other *newly*-Dominating minds the mental paradigm preceding theirs. But if we want an impression of how people like us, adult human beings, engaged and interpreted life while amid the mood of Contention, we have one more hint besides our uninitiated children, and a tantalizing hint it is -- The ancient cave paintings.

There was a honeymoon period after humans entered into the mood of Domination but before that mood ripened into societies that would Dominate humans themselves. During that honeymoon period, Beth's contemporaries painted astonishing representations from their lives, where, still culturally fresh from the mood of Contention, they left possible insights into how a physically and intellectually modern human might perceive the world were she allowed to remain the wild human animal she was born.

This was the Original Elizabeth, she who predated even the cave paintings, instead of she of the informative classroom speech. We see how a vitality and a dynamism electrified the Original Elizabeth's world. We see her awed by her environment, by its exhilarating and forbidding power, even overwhelmed by it. The Original Elizabeth seems to have viewed nature and its creatures with the most intimate respect, but also with a sublime wonder. It is also possible she identified with these creatures in some way, felt them to be her equals in competition, just another wild animal like her, somewhat bigger, maybe, somewhat differently intelligent.

And those cave paintings suggest the Original Elizabeth as thoroughly and vigorously inhabiting the world that encompassed her; fully integrated into its ecosystem, part and parcel of its whole-ness, not selected out, separate. This implies the Original Elizabeth as integral to her environment, and as shaping its equilibrium as significantly as any other species, and as thriving in it when most emphatically herself -- a self-aware human animal. That ancient world had molded the Original Elizabeth into the being she was. Urgently and without cease it stimulated her to persist and flourish as that being. And so, as she engaged this environment which had created her and which continued to exist through her, the Original Elizabeth, by definition, could only move in a state of pristine self-expression. She was in perfect balance with her world, in complete spiritual harmony. She was herself, fully. She could not be herself more fully amid any other setting. Elizabeth moved in a peace, a wholeness, a oneness.

So take her fully integrated and acute human sensibilities, saturate them with a world of fiery and awe-inspiring natural stimulation, add the vibrating freedom and immediacy and joy we find in the behavior of our uninitiated children, and we have an outline of our original psychology, of our original relationship with the world. Vitality defined it, and an expansive grandness, and an incorruptible primal innocence.

And I do not believe this description to be too idealistic. For it is exactly, in fact,

the state of being that all the prophets
promise we will discover once we become
again purely and fully ourselves.